God, could you talk a little louder?

The Father of a Dying Son Struggles with His Faith

Tom J. Logue

Kent Popular Press

FOREWORD

It has been so painful to read again the notes I jotted down during Tommy Logue's 17 years with us that I have continually put off reading them again. But the unfinished business of preserving them for others has remained with me.

There have been a few friends who have pressed me, and I appreciate their insistence. The one thing that made me know I had to publish the material, however, was a statement Tommy wrote in an English paper his teacher gave us after his death. In the paper, he said he hoped he would write a book one day.

Tommy, this is your book!

Dad

Tommy Logue (1955-1972)

Chapter 1 _____

His cup
was measured
and he savored
every drop.

THE FAMILY

Tom, born October 8, 1921, in Waco, Texas

Ethel, born August 18, 1926, in Memphis, Tennessee

Louise, born October 31, 1951, in Memphis, Tennessee

Tommy, born January 15, 1955, in Memphis, Tennessee

Tim, born October 7, 1956, in Little Rock, Arkansas

John, born February 20, 1958, in Little Rock, Arkansas

FIRST BORN

Ethel and I left the house in a hurry and in the rain. I am glad 1939 Nelson in Memphis is close to Baptist Hospital. We were both pretty nervous.

We have our first child, Margaret Louise Logue. I am glad to get a girl. Dr. Taylor said she was completely healthy, and that is all that really matters. But she is beautiful, too.

Some of our Memphis State students, Helen Singleton, Eva Jane Wallis, Carolyn Brashear, Bill Jones, and Harold Bay, have already given her a nickname -- "Spooks" -- because of her Halloween birthday.

October 31, 1951

DIFFICULT, TENNESSEE

Ethel and I dropped our Louise by Ethel's brother's in Lafayette, Tennessee, on our way to Ridgecrest, North Carolina. As we were making our way back to the main highway, my eyes fell upon a signpost for two nearby Tennessee towns. One arrow said "Difficult 2 miles." The other said "Defeated 4 miles."

As we drove on toward Ridgecrest, my mind was back at the signpost. Why would people name their town "Difficult?" Why would anyone name his town "Defeated?"

I wondered if there were a Baptist church at either town. In my mind's eye I could see the signs: "The Difficult Baptist Church" . . . "The Defeated Baptist Church." I had seen both varieties of churches, but I had never seen signs "tell off" on a church like that before.

And then the inevitable question: Does anyone ever move from Defeated to Difficult or from Difficult to Defeated? Either way, it is just two miles. But what a difference in attitude. What a difference in philosophy and theology.

I knew which town I would prefer to live in. I'd be a proud citizen of Difficult. I'd vote in every election. I'd sweep its streets. I'd paint its fences.

I knew the Logues could make it in Difficult, but I knew that none of us could ever make it in Defeated.

June, 1953

Our son, Tommy, was born today at Baptist Hospital in Memphis. His grandmother, suffering from stomach ulcers, is a patient in the same hospital. So, I have "commuted" between Ethel's room and Mrs. Garrott's room -- that is, when I am not in front of the nursery watching Tommy's every move.

It has been a special thrill to name this new son Tom J. Logue, Jr., and I hope he will always be as proud to be a Junior as I was to be one. It seemed to give me a special relationship to my dad. (Tommy would really be a "III" if my father were still living.)

I have been reminded of a big surprise in my family at the beginning of World War II. When I sought a birth certificate at the County Clerk's Office in Waco, Texas, I discovered my folks or the hospital or someone had failed to fill in my name. The certificate only read "boy baby Logue."

One of my friends, Bob Focht, never calls me Tom, only "boy baby Logue." Well, Tommy, at least you have a name to begin with.

January 15, 1955

DEAR GOD, COMMA

We have made our move from Memphis to Little Rock and are becoming real Arkansans. We love our house even though it it very small. I think we really bought the house because of the beautiful trees.

Today I woke the family with my laughter which floated easily from the front room to the three bedrooms. In my new position as State Student Director, I have a full time secretary for the first time. From day one I included punctuation in my dictation. I often wondered if I offended the secretary with this practice. Since I had graded English papers at Baylor as one of the ways to pay for college, I guess I have not wanted to run the risk of having to correct punctuation mistakes again.

So, as I started to pray this morning, I said, "Dear God comma . . . ." Ethel was not that pleased to be awakened and later put me in my place. "If I were God," she said, "I would have answered, Dear Tom (with a small t). Get to work . . . exclamation mark."

Undated

CRASHING OUR BAPTIST
STUDENT CONVENTION

Ethel called me at the motel in Conway about eight this morning. She was having labor pains and leaving for the hospital. I made the fastest trip to Little Rock from Conway that I have ever made. Not too long after I arrived, Dr. McCaskill came out of the delivery room to tell me we had another son. I relayed the news to the church office at First Baptist Church in Conway where our Baptist Student Convention was being held, so that our students and directors could know of the safe arrival of Timothy Garrott Logue. Garrott is Ethel's maiden name.

Our churches speak of new members as "additions." So welcome, Timothy, to the human race and to the Logue clan. You are a welcome "addition," even if you did crash our Baptist Student Convention.

October 7, 1956

A TELEGRAM FROM IKE

I think everyone attending the Baptist Student Convention was as thrilled as was Dale Jones, our convention president, when he received a wire sent from the White House at 4:00 p.m. on October 11, 1957. The wire to Dale says:

Please give my greetings to the members of the Baptist Student Union of Arkansas meeting in their annual convention.

With the vigor of youth, inspired by the wisdom of the ages, you are accomplishing great things for good. Out of your worship and discussions, I am sure you will gain strength to advance the service of God and neighbor.

Best wishes to you all,

Dwight D. Eisenhower

October 12, 1957

STUDENTS HOLD THEIR GROUND

Hooray for youth!

Our Arkansas Baptist State Convention closed its meeting several days ago. The resolutions which were passed said nothing about Central High being closed, nothing about the problem of segregation, etc.

But our students had done better and addressed the problem.

The student convention met in October in Jonesboro, where First Baptist Church served as host. I was proud of our students who passed as one of their resolutions a strong statement on race relations. The resolution was approved at a meeting of the state council at breakfast Saturday morning before it was presented to the full convention. We always invite the program personnel to the breakfast, and one of these, a pastor, strongly urged the state council not to present the resolution to the convention.

But the students, led by the state president, Dale Jones of the University of Arkansas, calmly went ahead and presented the resolution. It passed with only one dissenting vote. The resolution stated:

> We believe that the Christian position in the matter of race relations includes:
>
> 1. Upholding the teaching and example of Jesus regarding the equal worth of all individuals regardless of race, color, or station in life.
>
> 2. Upholding the law of the land.
>
> 3. Abstaining from and discouraging violence in the settlement of any differences.

November 26, 1957

MOVE OVER, TOMMY AND TIMOTHY

Our fourth child, John William, was born today at Baptist Hospital. Dr. McCaskill delivered John as he had Tim. Poor Louise was so disappointed that she had failed again to secure a little sister. She slammed down the phone at the house when I called to tell her of John's birth, but before that she said, "Just leave him there. Don't bring him home."

"Don't take it too seriously, John; she'll get over it. For one thing, she will still be able to have a room to herself. This may not mean much to her now, but it will later on.

"Welcome aboard, John William. Your arrival means you three guys have just one bedroom between you. Move over, Tommy and Timothy."

February 20, 1958

LIKE A BAD DREAM

For some time now Ethel and I have been worried about our oldest son, Tommy. He seems to wobble as he runs, and he has trouble climbing steps. His younger brother Tim runs much better. To get up from the floor, Tommy has to "climb" up his legs with his two hands.

While Ethel and I were in Nashville last month, Ethel's folks in West Memphis took Tommy to Campbell's Clinic in Memphis. The clinic's letter to us suggests that he has muscle retardation, cerebal palsy, or muscular dystrophy, but probably it is muscular dystrophy. I have looked up the words in the dictionary, and the possibility of muscular dystrophy is especially frightening.

To think this could happen to our Tommy seems like a terribly bad dream.

June, 1959

TURNIPSEED KIN

We are in Gulf Shores, Alabama, again. We try to come to the Gulf each year. As usual, our Turnipseed cousins have come to visit us while we are here. Nadine and Sammie C. live in Troy; and Minnie Rae and her husband, Johnny, live in Fairhope. Nadine and Sammie C. have never married. All of them have "adopted" our four children and are special, special people.

My father's mother and father both died before he was a year old, and he was raised by his grandparents, also named Turnipseed. The girls tell me that my dad went as a "Turnipseed" until he was 12 when he decided to use his actual name "Logue."

In my family, when one says, "that's the Turnipseed in you," he is referring to the sentimental and emotional part of one of us. Most of us Logues have a lot of Turnipseed in us.

I have had fun through the years telling people my dad's mom was a Turnipseed. But the truth is we Logues are very much Turnipseeds also.

Summer, 1961

WELCOME HOME!

Today Tommy and Ethel came back from Mayo's. Basically, it was a good trip, she said. Tommy had his medical appointments in the morning, and in the afternoon they shopped and went to shows. There is no change in the diagnosis.

Ethel said that the clinic wanted to hospitalize and keep Tommy a week longer, doing the muscle biopsy among other tests. But she felt they wanted him to stay for research more than anything. Ethel said it really embarrassed Tommy to be stripped to his shorts with seven or eight doctors talking about his condition as he was stretched out on a bed.

I felt pretty proud of myself, taking care of things while Ethel was gone. Our wonderful helper, Sarah Strong, did her share, of course.

But my pride didn't last too long. At the airport, Ethel noticed immediately that I had put the wrong shoes on John -- the right shoe on the left foot and the left shoe on the right foot. And he never complained. He was probably too excited about getting his mother and brother home again.

July 12, 1963

AN AD IN THE NEW YORK TIMES

The more we have read about muscular dystrophy the more we have realized what a cruel disease it is. The pseudohypertropic type, which Tommy has, manifests itself early in young boys. Stated in simple terms, muscular dystrophy keeps the body from absorbing protein. Most of the victims of this type die in their teens. All of the muscles in the body weaken, and most of the victims die of heart or lung difficulties.

A medical breakthrough or a miracle from God is our only hope. I've done a lot of reading on non-medical healings of different sorts. Some are well documented. I've also attended fairly regularly the healing services at Christ Episcopal Church.

I ran an ad in the personal section of the New York Times recently urging muscular dystrophy researchers to hurry, for time was running out for an Arkansas couple and their son. Perhaps no researcher even saw the ad, but at least I was doing something.

Undated

A NATION IN GRIEF

It was difficult to speak today. I was the guest speaker at First Baptist Church at Lonoke, Arkansas. Of course, I was invited before President Kennedy was assassinated, and being the emotional person that I am, I had carefully prepared what I was going to say about the tragedy. In fact, I read that part when I was introduced.

Then I read the scripture and got into the sermon. A couple of older ladies on my right caught my attention. They were dabbing their eyes with their handkerchiefs. I must have paused for thirty seconds to get control of my own emotions again.

The nation is in grief, and each family has its own ritual. Tommy is the one most crushed in our family.

November 22, 1963

THE "M" ENCYCLOPEDIA

We have never used the term "muscular dystrophy" with Tommy. We have wondered many times if he has ever read of the disease in newspapers or magazines. On Labor Day weekends we watch the Jerry Lewis Telethon after he has gone to bed and make sure the TV is off during the day.

By insisting that he stay in regular school with his friends, he has avoided seeing people with his disease and others with physical difficulties who attend special education classes.

Recently, in looking up a phone number, Tommy saw, in my handwriting, "Muscular Dystrophy Association" and the accompanying phone number for our state office. He asked John for the "M's" in the encyclopedia.

Now he knows and we know he knows. He has memorized sentences in the short encyclopedia synopsis and quotes them to us.

How thoughtless of me! Why didn't I just use initials?

Undated

A HEALING PRAYER

Last Thursday afternoon, I returned to Christ Episcopal Church again for a healing service. The Rector, Rufus Womble, chatted with me awhile at the close. Ethel carried Tommy with her this weekend to pick up the little car his granddad, Mr. Garrott, had made for him. She talked with him on the way about the new arrangements that Mrs. LeMay, the principal, wants at school.

Tonight, while the rest of the family was at church, Tommy and I had a wonderful time together. We talked about the problem of his muscles, and I attempted talking about God's healing power. I wrote on a card the three parts of Rufus' prayer: "Thank You, God, for Your healing power at work within me. Thank You, God, for Your healing power at work in the lives of the other people here. Thank You, God, for Your healing power at work in all the world."

When I told Tommy how happy he had made us, the prettiest little sheepish smile passed over his face as he grabbed my tie affectionately. I hope I can hold that in my mind's eye forever.

January 3, 1965

MY MISSING GLASSES

I visited friends last week in Hot Springs who had lost a family member. When I returned home, I realized I didn't have my eyeglasses. I called back to see if I might have left them at the house. I was told they could not find my glasses. There was an extra pair on the piano, but they were sure those belonged to the deceased.

At the graveside service, I served as a pallbearer. When the casket was opened it looked to me -- without my glasses -- that the deceased was wearing my glasses!

After the service was over, I asked the preacher to tarry with me a moment. I told him my dilemma.

Even looking closer, without my glasses, I couldn't tell for sure if the gentleman had on my glasses.

My glasses never have "shown up here" at the house, or the office, or anywhere.

My guess is they have "shown up There." Well, if they had to go, I am glad they didn't take me with them.

Undated

AN INTERIM CHAIR

Tommy's last year at Hardin Bale School is a year of transition. He is in the sixth grade and has been falling so often that we know he needs to be in a wheelchair. But it is so difficult for us to talk to Tommy about a wheelchair that we have worked out a substitute way for this year.

I get Tommy on my back and back up to the front seat of our car and strap him in. Then at the school, one of his friends pushes out a teacher's chair that is on rollers. I move Tommy from the car to the chair, and his friend rolls him into class.

There is no question that we will soon need a wheelchair. But I am grateful for this interim, this compromise. It postpones, for a while, the trauma of the use of a wheelchair.

October, 1965

DR. FRANK LAUBACH'S VISIT

Dr. Frank Laubach, a world renowned literacy expert, is speaking at our Baptist Student Convention. He asked to stay in a home rather than in a motel.

In a short time, he has become a part of the family. He asked Ethel to wash some of his clothes. At supper last night, the boys started telling elephant jokes, and he roared with laughter, bringing out our youngest and most timid child, John, who also had to tell his favorite elephant joke.

At bedtime, Dr. Laubach asked us to have prayer together. As Tommy was already in bed, we clasped hands around his bed, and as we did, Dr. Laubach said, "God is speaking all the time, all the time, all the time. And we need to be listening all the time, all the time, all the time."

Lord, I am trying to listen. What are you telling me about Tommy and through Tommy?

December 2, 1965

GOD, COULD YOU TALK A LITTLE LOUDER?

I have such a hard time understanding pain and suffering and especially incurable diseases in a young person such as Tommy.

About the only thing that really helps me is to realize what havoc would happen on earth if all of our prayers were answered. Life would become too simple also. If I had a headache, I would get rid of it with a prayer. If my tomatoes were not doing too well, I would make them strong and vibrant with a prayer.

"What are You trying to say to us, Lord? Lord, it's a question mark this time and not a comma. And while I am on the subject, Lord, could You speak a little louder?"

Undated

CARMELITES MAKE GOOD NEIGHBORS

The Carmelite Sisters are just two doors from us, but several centuries away from us, I thought at first.

When we moved into the neighborhood, their bells woke me while it was still dark. I wanted to ask the sisters if they needed to wake up the whole neighborhood when they start whatever the first thing they do every day. But, I didn't.

Sister Catherine is the one who is not cloistered. She sees about all the physical things of the place. It was she who invited our three boys inside their place. Being a Baptist preacher, I quizzed the boys thoroughly about what went on inside the walls.

I can't believe those sweet sisters let those three Protestant boys sort the altar bread. The sisters forgot to make them wash their hands. Surely Vatican II has not thrown out belief in germs.

And then Christmas came, and Sister Catherine brought us two loaves of homemade bread. Our Catholic neighbors are orthodox after all, I have discovered. They believe in tradition. The loaves of bread have kept coming every year.

And best of all, Sister Catherine always whispers that they pray for Tommy every day.

Undated

PRESSURE ON THE MARRIAGE

We have employed our first part-time worker with muscular dystrophy patients in Arkansas, Virginia Henker. She visits in the homes of the patients and shares details of what is provided by the Muscular Dystrophy Association and also gives suggestions to parents about handling everyday problems. By going from home to home, she learns of different solutions that parents have discovered.

It would be so helpful if we could find and could afford a male nurse who could stay with the patients while the parents get away for a few days together. I bumped into Charles Petty in Philadelphia recently, and he told me about the elevated divorce rate among muscular dystrophy parents. I had suspected this because, as state president of the Muscular Dystrophy Association, I had been amazed at the number of couples who divorce even before the child dies. I think some of these marriages could have been saved given time for retreat and intimacy.

With all that the young patients have to endure, it seems so cruel that they also be faced with a feeling of guilt when their parents separate. I know that Tommy's condition has taken its toll on Ethel's and my relationship. In discussing this with male friends, several have first said they would stay with Tommy, but when the details of what that would involve in the way of caring for his personal needs are discussed, they have dropped the subject. And I would probably react the same way if the roles were reversed.

Dick Norton and George Amos are exceptions, however. Both have volunteered to stay with Tommy.

Undated

FLYING AIRPLANE TICKETS

Glyn Finley, our student director at Arkansas Tech, and Winston Hardman, our student director at University of Central Arkansas, are helping me carry Tommy to the Christian Life Commission meeting in New York City. We flew into Buffalo, rented a car, and will go to see Niagra Falls tomorrow.

As soon as we checked into our hotel in Niagra Falls, Ontario, I raised a window to get some fresh air. Immediately, our airplane tickets, which were on the window sill, flew out. Glyn rushed down to retrieve them while I stood guard from our fifth floor window. Tommy told me I had better let him take care of the tickets in the future.

Tommy wondered if airplane tickets had ever "flown" that far before without their passengers. "Tickets without passengers are as bad as passengers without tickets," he said.

April, 1966

MEETING ARTHUR GOLDBERG

Glyn Finley is having the time of his life here in New York City. From Fordyce, Arkansas, Glyn has not seen the sights of the city before. He is amazed at the city being open 24 hours. His "night" life, plus doing most of the carrying of Tommy on his back, is about to get the best of him. Winston and I, both a bit older, have been to New York before but are thoroughly enjoying Glyn's and Tommy's reactions.

Dr. S. A. Whitlow, Executive Secretary of our Arkansas Baptist State Convention, is here with his wife. Today, he told us that we could always go to church on Sunday night but that we could not always see a hockey game at Madison Square Garden. That is all it took for Glyn to take off for the hockey game.

The biggest thrill of the trip was our meeting Arthur Goldberg, our Ambassador to the United Nations. He came up and introduced himself to us. Perhaps Tommy's being on Glyn's back caught his attention. Goldberg is one of the speakers at our conference which is being held in a building just across the street from the United Nations.

April, 1966

THEOLOGY 101

The boys and I are taking a few days off, staying in Jack and Linda Patterson's trailer at Mountain Harbor and swimming in the pool.

It has been a theological day. I have been reading Tournier's The Meaning of Persons and sharing with the boys some of the thoughts of the book. This morning, we took sheets of paper and wrote down our thoughts. Later, I volunteered to go over anyone's thoughts, but I didn't have any takers.

As we took Tommy for a stroll in his wheelchair, Tim asked, "Is it God's fault that there's sin in the world?" He continued to probe. "Would there have been sin if Adam hadn't eaten the apple? If there wasn't a God, would there still be sin in the world?"

Then he made a theological deduction of his own. God must have made other people the same time He made Adam or everyone's name today would be Adam -- like Logue, if we had been the first family upon the earth.

While Tim and John were swinging, Tommy asked me why I give him vitamin E. I told him that his body doesn't seem to absorb vitamin E. He wanted me to give him more.

When Tim and John took the empty cereal cartons and bowls back into the trailer, Tommy asked me, "How long should I live?" I was not sure he was asking me what I was afraid he was asking.

"How long will I live -- as long as you?" he asked.

"Most generations live longer than the past generation," I replied.

"Yeah, but how about me . . . 60 years . . . 30 years?" And smiling, he continued, ". . .12 years?" He wanted me to ask the doctor.

"But I'd rather ask God," Tommy said.

Summer, 1967

SLAIN IN THE SPIRIT

Going to San Francisco, I went by Laguna Beach to see my Aunt Fannie Gene. While there, I noticed an advertisement for a service to be conducted in Los Angeles by Kathryn Kuhlman, an evangelist who holds healing services.

So after my San Francisco meeting, I came back through LA so I could attend the service. The church was so packed I had to go to the balcony to find a seat.

The service was "strong" . . . real strong, quite a contrast to the quiet and dignified healing services at Christ Episcopal in Little Rock I attend. But if anything could help Tommy or me, I was game.

I was surrounded by Four Square Gospel people attending the closing session of their convention I learned.

I tried to relax. Surely there was no Southern Baptist there who would rat on me.

Eventually, people were invited to come to the altar where Miss Kuhlman touched their foreheads. Quite a few just fell backwards when touched. Fortunately, someone caught them.

I decided to go for the whole experience. But if I fell backwards, would anyone catch me, a Southern Baptist? I found my way to the front. Eventually, Miss Kuhlman touched me also. I was ready for anything, but I didn't fall out. I was sort of disappointed.

When I returned to the balcony, I was soon shocked when everyone, it seemed, gave a long and ascending "oh . . .," inhaling 99% of the oxygen in the place. But I had enough oxygen to ask my neighbor, "What was that all about?"

"That is Brother McPherson," he said, "the pastor of this church and the son of Aimee Semple McPherson. He's just been slain in the spirit."

I knew I wanted, and needed, something extra in my life, but I was not sure I was ready to be slain.

Nevertheless, I do believe in non-medical healings and do believe in the ministry of people like Kathryn Kuhlman.

February 14, 1968

THE SIZE OF THE DREAM

Martin Luther King has been killed.

This man, who always advocated non-violence, has been himself the victim of violence.

All of us state student directors are meeting in Callaway Gardens in Georgia. Tonight, after our session, five of us drove into Atlanta to pass by the casket at Ebenezer Baptist Church to pay our respects. The streets were packed.

W. F. Howard, the Texas director, said, "Can you believe the profound quiet in the streets, despite the many, many small children with their parents?"

Bill Jenkins, the Virginia director, was impressed, as was I, with the warmth and acceptance of the members of Ebenezer Baptist who served sandwiches and drinks in the basement of the church. As Bill said, to experience the deep and expansive grief of the masses, who were standing in the long line for the better part of the night, is something that we can never forget.

Reverence.

And we were reverent as we drove back to Callaway Gardens.

As was Tommy in Little Rock.

And I thought of what Gary Thrailkill had said to me, "It's not so much the size of the man that makes the dream come true, but the size of the dream that makes the man come true."

April 9, 1968

SOMEONE TO LOVE ME

"I'm already 14, and when I'm 16 everyone will be going to proms, and when I'm 18 everyone will have a car, and when I'm 21 everyone will be married, and no one will ever love me."

"Sure, someone will love you," I said.

"Oh, I don't mean cousins and aunts and uncles," Tommy said.

Summer, 1968

FOOD VERSUS HEREDITY

Our three boys' height is very important to them. Their five feet, six and a half inch daddy is not much of an inspiration, I fear. Tommy wants to be measured in bed. Tim is doing his own measuring with a pencil mark on the wall.

Recently, Tim asked me if I knew how he could become taller. I took advantage of the situation and suggested less sweets, more fruits and vegetables, and more exercise.

He has been taking my good advice, but his growth is still very slow. I see his disappointment as he measures himself on the wall again and again.

Today he confronted me and said, "Dad, it's food versus heredity, and heredity is going to win out." It was Tim's nice way of saying, "Dad, really it's all your fault."

Undated

THE DEATH OF DREAMS AND HEROES

Our nation is in shock again. Robert Kennedy has been assassinated. If possible, Robert Kennedy was even more of a hero for Tommy than John Kennedy.

Tommy was almost nine when John Kennedy was killed but didn't feel that strongly about the cause of peace, feeding the hungry people of the world, or of eradicating racial prejudice then.

But now that he is thirteen, Tommy is keenly interested in social issues. He is vitally interested in sports, too, and for years Sandy Koufax of the Los Angeles Dodgers has been a hero for him. But, Robert Kennedy is in a class by himself, and Tommy is terribly depressed.

June 5, 1968

MOTHER IS 85

My mother, that is. And Joe's and Dorothy's and Helen's and Elizabeth's and Bill's mother, too. In fact, she was a mother another time. She and daddy lost their first child, Louise.

Mother's middle name was Perkle. I never did tell anybody that. I was ashamed of it, really. It sounded too much like Pinkham, as in Lydia Pinkham. Or maybe a name that would be good for a brand of coffee.

I am not ashamed of mother, though. She is something else. I always thought if any of us kids ever wrote a book on mother, we ought to call it the Widow's Might. Mrs. Gurley, who taught me at Singer Avenue or West Junior High in Waco, was always using that phrase.

Mother was tough, maybe in a mild sort of way. She did the discipline in the family. My brother, Bill, and I used to tell her she would never have peaches on the peach tree if she did not quit whipping us with so many of those peach tree limbs.

When the depression hit and dad lost the cotton market and the grocery store and the house we lived in and his own health for awhile, mother kept the family going.

I did not always agree with what we could afford and could not afford. I would have saved on the water bill and on the soap bill by not taking so many baths. I was not for quitting Lux or Palmolive and going for mom's homemade lye soap. I missed Ipana toothpaste when we moved to salt and soda. I did not mind Billy Symes, from across the street, seeing our "poverty" because the Symes did not have much money either. Billy would go down the alley with us Logue boys to find Jones Fine Bread wrappers so that we could get in free at the Kiddie's Matinee at the Waco Theatre on Saturdays.

If kids at the other schools in Waco knew some of us at Sanger Avenue School had quit using Ipana toothpaste and Lux soap maybe they would have stopped calling us the "Sanger Avenue Silk Sox Sissies" at all the ball games.

February 22, 1969

P.S. Mother lived to be 101.

KIDS' NIGHT AT RAY WINDER FIELD

I took the boys to the Arkansas Travelers baseball game tonight. Tommy and I hurried back to the van to get ahead of the crowd while Tim and John and Tim's friend, Tim Walker, waited for the drawing for free bicycles, watches, and most of all -- a free pony. It was "Kids' Night" at Ray Winder Field.

While we were waiting, Tommy complained that many of the kids would stare at him and his wheelchair, and he asked if it was okay if he stared back. He admitted that the reason he stared back was so they would feel stupid too.

But Tommy was not real happy with himself for the times he had stared. "I ought to be more mature than that, daddy," he confessed.

June 19, 1969

DO I TELL THE TRUTH?

As I lay in bed with Tommy a few minutes today and scratched his seat and back, he asked again about the preacher in Mississippi who has muscular dystrophy. I knew he was fascinated with the idea of a man who had lived that long. Tommy asked if the man had a family. I could sense his delight in learning of children.

But then my problem. Should I tell him the truth -- that the preacher had an adult kind of muscular dystrophy and that it had struck him later in life?

Well, I did. And then there was a terrible silence, and I knew some air castles had fallen for Tommy. After awhile, he said, "Daddy, I'm going to be a sex maniac." I laughed and asked why. "Because girls will never like me, and there won't be anything else to do."

I had a big laugh and after some more silence, he said, "I'm just going to fall in love with pictures, not real people."

Trying to change the subject, I said, "Let's have a great day together. What had you rather do than anything in the whole wide world?"

"Not having a great day with you," he was quick to answer with a smile.

June 21, 1969

JOHN AND TOMMY

John gives of himself so completely to Tommy. It concerns us, for we fear that he is not developing his own relationships outside the home.

John comes straight home from school and stays in the room with Tommy, moving his books, helping him get more comfortable in the wheelchair, changing the TV channel, etc.

No brother ever had a better brother than John. What if we had known earlier that Tommy had MD and decided not to have any more children?

On the average, one out of every two males born to a mother who is a muscular dystrophy carrier has the disease. How fortunate we are that our other two sons do not have the disease.

And, how fortunate for Tommy that we did not know he had the disease and went ahead and had two other healthy boys.

God knew Tommy needed younger brothers. I am glad He looked after us in this when we did not even know He was.

Undated

SPITTIN'

"Daddy, I need to talk to you.

"You know I get to arguing, and Tim and John won't listen to my explanation, and I get mad and spit, and they spit back.

"I can't hit anyone. So I spit instead of beating them up. It's just like being a bully.

"Daddy, is it bad to spit at people?"

October 29, 1969

GOD VERSUS TJL?

The Arkansas/Texas football game of 1969 determined the national championship. It was the 100th year of football, and Richard Nixon and Billy Graham were at the game. Arkansas led most of the game, 14-0, only to be defeated in the last quarter, 15-14. Most Arkansans were very depressed. A couple who listened to the game with us confessed that they had to take sleeping pills to go to sleep that night.

Our children were depressed also, as were we, and out of the loss of the game Tommy asked lots of questions about God's will. "Daddy, did our loss mean that the Texas football team was composed of better people?" he asked. Being a former Texan, I was pondering that question when Tommy asked an even more difficult one. "Did God want us to lose that game, daddy?"

I assured Tommy that if God did want Arkansas to lose that game, for the number one spot in the country, God and I had never been on opposite sides more clearly.

Fall, 1969

PROCRASTINATION

It's Christmas time again, and the kids know how I feel. It is just not my favorite time of the year. I hate the extra traffic and the mad dashing around and all the commercialism.

Ethel and Lou love it, and they call me "Scrooge."

Tommy has done his own thinking about Christmas. A lot of it is good theology.

"Daddy, we give to Santa Claus the attributes of God, don't we?" Tommy asked one day.

"What do you mean, son?"

"You know -- those three omni things." I soon realized he was talking of omnipresent, omnipotent, and omniscient.

"When we were little, you and mom used to tell us to be good because Santa was watching. And the song says, Santa knows when we are bad or good, so we ought to be good for goodness sake. It seems to me that the one concerned about how we act is God and not man-made Santa."

"I agree 100%, Tommy," I said.

"And we emphasize the wrong things so often," he said.

"Like what?" I asked.

"Like gifts instead of the gift of Jesus," he replied.

"Tommy," I said, "you ought to be helping me with my sermons."

"I would, dad, if you didn't wait till Saturday night to start working on them."

December, 1969

OLD AGE

Today as I was dressing Tommy, he said what he has said so many times, "I'm gross looking today, daddy." His thin shoulders and small body worry him so much.

"No, you're not, Tommy, you are good looking," I said.

He repeated the fact of his being "gross," and each time I would insist that he was good looking.

Finally, in desperation, I said, "Okay, have it your way. But look at me. I'm ugly, but I've still made a living for your mom and you four kids."

Then quick as a flash, but with no thought of hurting me, he said, "Yeah, dad, but it's okay for you to be ugly. You're old and you haven't got long to live."

Undated

LISTENING

Tonight, when I came home from work, I was unusually tired, was depressed about Tommy, and was also absorbed with some problems in my work. Our middle son, Tim, said something to me. I was looking at him, but not listening. Soon, it was clear that it had been a question, and I had not responded.

All of a sudden, Tim put his little hands on his hips and said, "Okay, dad, just stand there like a statue."

That awoke me. I was doing something I declared as a grade school boy I would never let happen. I was looking and not listening. My buddy, Harold, used to do that to me.

Tonight my prayer came logically in four parts:

> Lord, help me to listen to Ethel so I will be a better husband;
>
> Lord, help me to listen to my children so I will be a better father;
>
> Lord, help me to listen to students so I will be a better Student Director;
>
> Lord, help me to listen to Thee, so I will be a better disciple.

Undated

TOMMY'S OLDER FRIENDS

Tommy is fortunate in having several older friends. Rezy Mobarak, our friend from Iran, comes over often to play chess with Tommy. Rezy also has taken Tommy to many of the Southwest Junior High and Parkview High School basketball and football games.

Jerry Hodge helped me take the boys to Six Flags, and Gerald Cound helped me with Tommy when the boys and I went to Mexico City. Darrell Coleman served as "astrologer" at Tommy's last birthday party. Bill Holman brought over his homemade cherry pie afterwards.

Another older friend of Tommy's is Paul Meers, a member of the Arkansas House of Representatives. Paul is full of stories and, tonight during a chess game, I overheard him tell Tommy one of the funniest stories I have ever heard him tell.

Paul told of seeing two old mountain women walking on the outskirts of Mountain Home, Arkansas, one day. He stopped to see if they wanted a ride, and both of them got into the front seat with Paul.

"What do you call your name?" one of them asked.

"I'm Paul Meers," Paul answered.

"Are you any kin to Walter Meers?" the lady asked.

"Yes, he was my father," Paul answered.

"Well, young man, do you know if Walter ever got himself married?" she asked.

Undated

A GOOD LOOKING BOY

"Will I look worse when I get older?"

"No, I don't know anything else that could happen to you."

"When I'm passing in a car, can people tell something is wrong with me? I just don't want to look too weird. I'm not too weird looking am I, daddy?"

"No, son, you are a good looking boy."

Undated

Chapter 2 _____

And he runs through the
pasture of my memory,
and the wind of contentment
catches his hair.

THANKS, JERRY LEWIS

On Ethel's flight to Albany, New York, to see her friend, Rosa, she spotted Jerry Lewis on the plane. Because Jerry has done so much for research on muscular dystrophy, he is like a patron saint to parents of muscular dystrophy children. In fact, we have wondered if St. Jude's Hospital in Memphis should not be renamed "St. Jerry's."

I asked Ethel if she had spoken with Jerry. "No," she said, "I was afraid I couldn't control my emotions."

Thanks, Jerry, for everything. Someday, somewhere, researchers you have funded, as well as inspired, will find a cure. And children will walk and run, and the wind of contentment will catch their hair.

Undated

NO REAL FUN

Tommy has noticed that his friends are beginning to date. The other night, he said, "My friends are already beginning to date and in two years they will be driving a car on dates.

"If I ever have a date, it would have to be a double date with someone else driving the car. I never will get to be in a car with a girl by myself.

"I never can do anything fun -- like kissing a girl."

Undated

SPITTIN' AGAIN

When Tommy came home from school yesterday, he said the boy who had pushed him out to the car -- not his best friend, who usually does it -- had put a tall stack of books on top of his own. They fell off and the boy cursed. They fell off again, and the boy cursed some more. Each time he was blaming it on Tommy for not holding the books better. The third time he cursed Tommy, Tommy got so mad he spit at him. The boy spit back and said, "You'd better watch it. I'll mash your face in." A buddy of Tommy's standing by told the boy to cut it out.

In reflection, Tommy wanted to know why his buddy came to his rescue. Did his buddy think he was a weakling? I tried to assure him that this was a real friend coming to help him.

Tommy doesn't like to be thought of as a weakling and certainly does not like to be thought of as a "sweet" boy. He rather enjoys being cast in the role of someone doing something wrong.

February 18, 1970

LEAVING SOUTHWEST JUNIOR HIGH

Today, Tommy told me again how much he dreads completing school. He loves school and is sad at the thought of leaving Southwest Junior High. But he not only worries about leaving junior high; he worries about finishing high school and college.

Today he seemed to have found his solution. "I don't want to go to work somewhere. It won't be as much fun as school. I guess I'll just have to be a school teacher.

"Do you think I ought to go ahead and plan for the future like everyone else and not worry about it?"

"Yes."

"Okay, daddy, if you say so."

Undated

RABBI LOGUE

Two days ago, I performed the marriage ceremony for a girl from our church and a Jewish classmate; both are medical students at Tulane. I asked two different rabbis to help me with the service, but neither could help. So, I performed the service by myself.

The service was held in the backyard of the bride's parents. Only the family was there, but a next door neighbor obviously viewed the service from her kitchen window. She must have heard about the possibility of a Baptist/Jewish clergymen combination, for she told a mutual friend of ours at Safeway yesterday, "Did you know that Baptist preacher never did show up, and the poor rabbi had to do the service all by himself."

August 17, 1970

A "DEAR JOHN" LETTER

Tim got his first "Dear John" letter today. Though it hurt me to see him hurt, I thought the letter was hilarious:

> Tim, I think that note you wrote me was real sweet. [She had first written "sweat" and scratched through it.] I nearly cried in Geography. I have to tell you the truth. I felt terrible about it and wish Danny could have put it a different way. It's not all because you're short so don't feel bad about that. I like another boy and have since the middle of 6th grade. I hope that he likes me and I know you will like another girl by report card time. I'm sorry I had to lead you on so much. I really didn't mean for it to go that far.
>
> Susan

John could not understand why it was called a "Dear John" letter when it was not even addressed to him.

Tommy's only comment was, "I wish I had a real girl friend even if we did break up."

Undated

THE WHEELCHAIR

In dressing Tommy today, he was again asking me some very difficult questions.

He started again with the wheelchair, which always seems to be the focal point. Rather soon, he was asking me how long he had to live. He wanted a specific answer. Was it two years? Was it ten years? He saw no reason for going to school if he did not have long to live.

"Are people nice to me just because I'm in a wheelchair?" He wants so desperately to be treated just as a person for what he is.

Tommy asked me if I remembered the black boy in his class. "I would never think of talking to him about the race problem," Tommy said. "No one ever thinks of his being any different from us. Could it be that that's the way they think about me? No one ever talks to me about the wheelchair." He had made a good analogy and wanted so very desperately for it to be true. I assured him that I thought it was true.

Again, he wanted to know if anyone would ever marry him. I answered by saying that there were a lot of women who marry men in wheelchairs. Then, Tommy expressed his fear that no one would really want to marry him because one would say, "I may love him too much and then he would just die and go away."

Undated

EIGHT LEGS

Tommy's English teacher, Mrs. Ladd Davies, shared an autobiographical paper he wrote for her class recently. The neatest sentence made fun of his own physical problems: "I am in a wheelchair, but that's because I have eight legs."

His humor showed in other places also: "By the way, I'm a boy, and I got it from my father," and "Someday I would like to get married -- for many decent reasons."

His rabid interest in sports was clear: "The most exciting moments in my life have probably had something to do with sports. Last year, Southwest Junior High played for the state championship in basketball and lost. The excitement I felt that game and in many others is unmatched."

Tommy mentioned trips we have made together, which pleased me, as well as stating how much he had enjoyed "all the foreign students I have met through my father's work . . . ."

The short two-page paper has revealed something about his faith. He speaks of "my decision to try to follow Christ" and closes the paper, "I want a happy life with some hard work and some pleasures. I will try not to make it boring and depressing like many people do. I think I have some important purpose, and I hope to find it. Last of all, I do want to go to a life after death."

October, 1970

STILL MINE

Thank you, God, for giving him to me another
    day, and
Though I have been gone all day
And tended to a million trivialities
Tonight in silent sleep he was mine.
And I touched him and made him move
Just to see that he was still mine
And I cried
Because I fear that life without the <u>wonder</u> of him
The <u>bother</u> of him
The <u>cry</u> of him
Will be
Empty
And I will curse myself for trying
To do Your work when I
Should have stopped and watched
The wonder of Your child.

1970

TOMMY'S WAY WITH WORDS

Several days ago, I was doing something for Tommy. I forget what it was, but he objected.

"It's for your own good," I said.

"I've been gooded all my life," Tommy retorted.

He never throws a word away. Recently, he said, "If you all ever die, leave me in my wheelchair." In a way, he hates the wheelchair, and yet he cherishes it because it carries him to everything he goes to in life.

Also recently, he said to me, "I'd rather have bad dreams than good ones. When I have bad dreams and wake up, I feel good. But, when I have good dreams and wake up, I feel bad." And I wondered if he dreamed of walking and running again.

Life is still precious to him. "Daddy, am I going to die soon? I don't want to miss anything. If I'm going to get there anyway, I don't want to hurry and miss anything here."

1970

12TH AND UNIVERSITY

It was a hot, humid day. My car is not air conditioned. I always go home the same way, from town to Battery to 12th to University. At 12th and University, I have to wait for a small green arrow telling me I can turn left. It seldom speaks. If I could add up all the time I have spent at 12th and University, it would total weeks of my life, it seems.

Tommy is not doing well. In a fast moment, I confronted God as I have never confronted Him before. Thoughts surfaced that had never surfaced before. Words came out that had never been used in my prayers before.

Lightning did not strike. I think I would have welcomed it. At least I would have known He was listening. The only noise was the lucky cars and trucks that had the green light on University.

I think for a few days I felt guilty, but then there was the knowledge that probably the 12th and University prayer was the most honest prayer of my life. I came to a new appreciation of what the Incarnation means. I came to understand a little better the question Jesus asked the Father from the cross.

And it all happened at 12th and University.

Undated

AFTER ALL THE BAD WORDS

Ethel and Elinor Royce went to Conway yesterday afternoon to get out of town for a little while. As I was putting Tommy to bed, he complained of his heart hurting, as he did this morning as we dressed. As we were unloading at school, he reminded me that we had forgotten the lunch. I went back home and brought him his lunch and went on to work. When I got to work, Marilyn Motley, the office secretary, told me that the school nurse had called to say that Tommy was sick. I rushed out to Parkview and found him nauseated and still with his heart hurting. He did not feel like going to the doctor, so we went home and rested. The doctor sent out some kind of relaxing medication.

After resting and sleeping for about an hour or so, Tommy said he was willing to go to the doctor's office. Dr. Briggs was immediately alarmed and told me that there was some infection and trouble in the sac around the heart. Tommy realized that something was wrong when the doctor called me out to talk in another room.

Ethel had come in by then, and she met us at the doctor's office. Tommy told Ethel, "I am sixteen years old and I need to know what is wrong with me."

I am back home tonight while Ethel stays at the hospital with him. They had a hard time drawing blood and never did really get a blood sample, but all the other tests were taken. We still do not know anything.

As we went toward the hospital from the doctor's office, Tommy said, "After you say all the bad words, there is nothing else to do but cry."

April 12, 1971

A STAY AT ARKANSAS CHILDREN'S HOSPITAL

This was Tommy's fourth day at Arkansas Children's Hospital. He came in on Tuesday.

I called my good friend Rufus Womble whose healing services at Christ Episcopal I have occasionally attended over the past ten years, and I asked him to come by and pray.

Rufus talked with us for awhile and then had Tommy repeat the scripture passage: "Peace I leave with you. My peace I give unto you . . . ." Then, he held one of Tommy's hands and put his other hand on Tommy's head and asked me to do the same.

Soon after Rufus left, Tommy went to sleep. On waking, he told me his heart had been beating heavily before Rufus came, but that after the prayer and nap it had slowed down.

Later I asked Tommy if he had repeated the "peace" scripture. He smiled and said, "yes" and gave me the peace sign with his two fingers.

April 23, 1971

SO UNINDEPENDENT

This has been a depressing day for Tommy. I suspect part of the problem is John's activities. Formerly, John seldom went out. But we are so grateful that now he goes out with friends, goes to parties, and has his own paper route. Both Tim and John went with friends to the State Fair today.

Tommy wanted me to roll him outside, and he was in a meditative mood. One of the things he said was, "I feel so unindependent. I can't do anything for myself. My parents have to go with me everywhere."

He asked if he had a Social Security number. He had been reading a pamphlet on scholarships, and there was something about Social Security in it. Tommy remarked that he would never need one because he would never have a job.

At one point, he said how much he wished he could drive a car and just go around and visit his friends. He also asked where the bath was upstairs and what color the curtains were in one of the bedrooms upstairs, and suddenly, it dawned on me he had never been upstairs.

I promised myself that I would get him upstairs soon.

October 2, 1971

THE GOD WHO WOULD IF HE COULD

"I have fasted, Lord. I have prayed. I have read everything on healing I can get my hands on.

"I have pleaded. I have begged. I have bargained. But, Tommy continues to deteriorate.

"I want to believe, Lord, You would -- if You could -- heal our boy. I really want to believe, Lord, that the question is not why don't You, but rather, why can't You?

"Early on, I was taught You were omnipresent, omniscient, and omnipotent. All of a sudden, I'm doubting Your omnipotence. If You could, if You would . . . but You won't . . . what kind of God are You, anyway?"

Undated

PLEASE SPEAK TO ME IN ENGLISH, LORD, AND NOT IN BAPTIST

Public prayer just is not one of my favorite things, hearing it or saying it.

We used to time Brother Odom's prayers at Seventh and James Baptist Church when I was a boy in Waco. He was a real stemwinder when it came to talking to the Lord in public.

I really do not like to be called on to pray in public. Sometimes my mind is 1,000 miles away, and I want so badly to say, "I pass."

Once, at the opening night service for all the BSU directors in the country, Dr. Kearnie Keegan called on me to pray. The next night, he did it again. I should have prayed, "Lord, ditto of last night's prayer." Sam Sanford, a student director from Louisiana, told me he was going to tell Dr. Keegan that I did not feel like I had done a good job in praying either night and that he thought I should have one more chance. And Sam is mean enough to do something like that. So I was plum ready the next night.

Most Baptists I have heard, pray in Baptist and not in English, like "we pray for those whom it is duty to pray for," or "lead, guide, and direct," or "return them to their much wanted health," etc. I would bet Methodists pray in Methodist and Presbyterians in Presbyterian.

"Lord, what are You trying to tell us about Tommy? Please speak to me in English, Lord, and not in Baptist."

Undated

MY GIFT FROM CHARLES ASHCRAFT

Today, I came home and stayed with Tommy a couple of hours while Ethel went to the beauty shop. Dr. Ashcraft, my boss, dropped by the house yesterday and told Ethel he wanted me to take off more. He came by the office also and said he wanted me to take a leave of absence, if I wanted to, for as many months as I felt that I needed. I told him I might need it later on more than now.

Back to the two hours I spent with Tommy. He wanted to be rubbed. Ever since he has been so very sick -- for about two weeks now -- he has not wanted people to touch him in any way. So many people dropping by has made him nervous, too. I have been tempted to put a sign outside the house and let people register their coming by but requesting them not to come in.

Today, Tommy spoke of life still having more times of feeling good than times of feeling bad. Somewhere in the conversation, he said something to the effect that it was good to get to die. I am sorry I didn't jot that down because I am not putting it in the beautiful language that he expressed it in.

Ethel's brother, Greer, and his wife, Jean, came over from West Memphis today with their two girls and spent the night with us. Greer had called the day before to see if they could come over, and I suggested that they make some excuse for the visit. Tommy has asked about all the company coming and wants to know if everyone is coming to tell him good-bye for the last time.

September 8, 1972

A TRUE RAZORBACK

Today was Ethel's and my anniversary. I ran early this morning, the first time I have gotten to run in a week or ten days. Greer and Jean left after lunch. I was supposed to be in Jonesboro last night and today, but I called Benny Clark, our student director at Arkansas State, and told him I couldn't make it.

Tommy has wanted to go to the Arkansas/University of Southern California ball game more than anything, and the doctor told him he could go. I was very opposed to it. If he could not go to school or church, etc., it looked sort of foolish to be going to a ball game. But anyway, we made it there and back amid the terrible traffic. I stayed at the BSU Center at the Med School with the van ready to come and get Ethel and Tommy if they needed me, but they stuck it out. USC beat Arkansas, 31-10.

Tommy was sort of philosophizing about his condition today. His chest has hurt him badly and he has had so much nausea with the medication that all his other complaints about looks and size have been minimized, and he said, "I guess not feeling so good is the only thing that is really wrong with me."

September 9, 1972

TAPS

Tommy had a rough night last night and as I was moving him around in the bed this morning so he would be more comfortable, I just stood there looking at him and loving him.

He opened his eyes and looked at me and smiled and said, "Why don't you just blow taps over me?"

September 11, 1972

A TRUE NEIGHBOR

Martha Hudson, our next door neighbor, has been so caring through the years and especially these last difficult weeks. She has almost daily brought over warm soup or other food, or sent a humorous card to Tommy. When someone suggested brandy for Tommy's coughing, it was this "Methodist" lady who begged brandy from the "Catholic" sisters for my "Baptist" family.

Martha has lessened her church activities, but her many deeds of kindness bring Christ into a lot of hungry and needy lives. And ours is one of them.

September 15, 1972

DAD

Our daughter Louise arrives from Crete today. We have been frantic, waiting for her return, hoping that Tommy would live until she came. He has asked about her as he has talked about his own death. We have made a few plans for the funeral, always hoping for the best. I wish I were strong enough to do the funeral myself. I think Tommy would want me to. He has been so strong himself in his struggle to live.

Today, his heart has had, for the first time, the irregular heart beat that they have warned us about. Dr. Briggs will come at noon today, and with him will be Mary Fuller, the lab girl at the clinic, who has been so fond of Tommy. It was in her wedding, held in our home several weeks ago, that Tommy served as best man.

I find myself doing little silly tasks around the house when I really want to be looking at him every second and touching him all the time, but he does not like anyone to touch him now. He is sleeping so poorly. He calls me "Dad" all the time, and it seems to me that he used to call me "Daddy." I wonder if even this is not an indication of just how tired he is in his fight to live.

September 27, 1972

LOU RETURNS

Louise arrived at 1:30 this morning. Her TWA plane to New York was late. She missed connections there and could only get as far as Memphis last night.

James Smalley arranged for Joe Sutherland to fly over to Memphis, and the two of them brought Louise back. She just hugged and kissed Tommy and cried over him. He was really glad to see her and smiled some. She was very talkative and I went up to her room and we talked until about 4:00. Later, when I was down in the bedroom praying, she walked in and said she wanted to just go and sit in Tommy's room awhile. She knocked over a trash can and woke up both Ethel and Tommy. Ethel invited her to sleep on the single bed with her.

Tommy is so very uncomfortable that I picked him up and rocked him. He was very embarrassed and was afraid someone would come in, but he was comfortable. He was embarrassed because he weighs only 77 pounds, embarrassed to be rocked at 17 years of age. I do not suppose I have rocked him in 15 years, but it was a good feeling for me to alleviate the pressure points on his body.

He was hurting even while we rocked. He said, "I wish someone would stab me." Then, when his mother came in the room, he asked, "How long do I have to be here?" Ethel acted as if she did not understand the question, and so he said, "You know, how long do I have to live? I am tired, tired, tired."

I do not think I ever heard Tommy use the word "invalid" before, but he used it this morning as we rocked, saying he didn't want to be an invalid the rest of his life.

Last night he felt well enough to talk about the future. He has felt so poorly that he has not even wanted to talk about school, but last night he wanted to know when we would make decisions about whether to drop some courses, whether to have a home-bound teacher, and whether to go ahead with the National Merit Scholarship.

"Lord, You've brought our family all together again. Unless Tommy's lingering and suffering is doing someone some good -- and even then, weigh it against what it is costing him -- help us to be ready to lose him."

September 28, 1972

CHANGING MY PRAYER

Today, Ethel came into the kitchen to get a pain pill. While she was fixing a Coke to go with it, I walked back into Tommy's room. He was speaking out loud.

I didn't know whether he was praying or whether he was saying words of a hymn. Several times I have heard him mumble in the oxygen tent and have asked him what he was doing. He has indicated that he was singing hymns.

When I asked him what he was saying, he yelled out at me not to ask him questions when he was in such pain.

If this pain continues, I cannot ask God to keep him alive.

October 3, 1972

HOSS' HAMBURGERS

Mary Arnold, the mother of Tommy's good friend, Ritter, called yesterday to say that they were coming over. I had written the Arnolds several days ago about the possibility of Ritter serving as a pallbearer. Ritter is in a private school in Alabama, and his parents had called him after receiving my letter to ask him if he would like to come on now. He told them he wanted to think about it, and had called later to say that he would.

They arrived this morning about 11:00, and called the house, and we acted as if it were all news to us. Tommy said that he did not want to see Ritter and got pretty emotional about it. We guess that it is because he did not want Ritter to see him in his present condition. When they came, Ritter did go on in. I do not know what conversation took place between them.

We invited the Arnolds to stay for lunch and they did. While Ethel, Jean, Bobbie Lee, and Louise ate lunch, I sat with Tommy. His conversation again was on death. He said to me that he wished that he could eat one of Hoss' grilled hamburgers, sip an orange drink and then just die. Or else he would like to get real hot and drink Koolaid and then die.

October 1, 1972

HELP MY UNBELIEF

Today I read some sentences which were found scratched on a basement wall by Allied Forces during the Holocaust. The victim's house had been destroyed, but not her spirit.

> I believe in the sun even when it doesn't shine.
> I believe in love even when it isn't shown.
> I believe in God even when He doesn't speak.

"God, help me to believe even when You refuse to speak. I can believe in the sun. I can believe in love. But I am having a hard time believing in You. Lord, I believe. Help thou my unbelief."

Undated

REMINISCING

Tommy is very, very low.

Kay Mosley, a nurse in our church, has been thoughtful enough to come help us with the suction pump. Tommy's face has been swollen the last couple of days, and he has just felt rotten.

He is cross with me most of the time and does not want me to touch him. I guess this helps me emotionally because this unusual "crossness" does keep me from hurting so much. I really relish the opportunity to help him turn or to go to the bathroom so that I can touch him again. I just pray as I touch him that he can gain some strength from me, both to live, as long as he can live, and strength to die when that comes.

Tommy has done a lot of reminiscing about the past, and perhaps this is a stage that one goes through. I have found the days similar in my own life. I thought back especially to my childhood and also to World War II days. Since his illness, I have finally, after 27 years, taken the time to write some of my old Army buddies. What a thrill it was to hear from Tom Billington, from New Bedford, Massachusetts.

Another interesting thing has been that there is a noise I hear that has reminded me for the first time in 45 years of the noise of the streetcar going up 18th Street and then turning down Sanger in Waco, Texas. I suppose it is actually the sound of trucks on University or on Boyle Park Road, but it sounds exactly like that noise of the streetcar when it would be climbing the hill, rocking back and forth, in Waco, Texas.

Tomorrow is Tim's birthday. I just thank God that Louise is with us. She has been such a strength since her arrival from Crete. How much worrying Tim and John do at school, I do not know. One of our next door neighbor boys, John Hudson, mentioned the fact that John was crying at school the other day.

October 6, 1972

A TOUGH LADY

God, never let me forget the beautiful patience and stamina of my wife as she waits on our dying child.

I will need to remember that later on. Don't let me ever forget.

Ethel really is tough. Without telling me, she went to the funeral home several weeks ago and made all the arrangements. She has had so much loss, so close together in her life. The loss of her father in 1965, the loss of a brother in 1967, and the loss of her mother in 1969.

And the toughest loss yet will soon be here.

October 8, 1972

OVERWHELMED

As I go to bed . . .
        Oh God! God! God!
That look of bewilderment, of lostness, like a scared child.
His swollen face.

I stood at the bed to tell him good night, and was so
overwhelmed I had to go to someone. So I raced upstairs to cry
with my other three flesh-of-my-flesh.

October 9, 1972

A TOUGH NIGHT

Last night was Tommy's most difficult night. He was in great pain and talked out of his head a great deal. It is the failure of the oxygen to get to his brain that causes this.

It was late Sunday night that a great emotion swept over me as I looked at him as he was going to bed. Ethel had him sitting up in bed, and I was standing at the foot. He had just taken his last pills, his face was swollen, and he looked up at me with the most pitiful expression in his eyes I have ever seen. The only way I can describe it is to compare it to the sight of a dog who has been beaten and is in a corner and looking up to see if one will strike again.

At this point I called Buddy Melton. We had a good talk, and Buddy offered a prayer for us over the phone. Then, I dialed Rufus Womble's Prayer for the Day. By then, I was more nearly ready to go to sleep, but the Lord had one other blessing for me. Ethel had fallen fast asleep, which is unusual with her that close to Tommy's bed. He needed help four or five times the next hour. I sat in a chair in the room and was able to help him each time, and this gave me a great comfort. The last time I helped him, Ethel woke up and insisted that I go back to our room.

Tommy is taking food now, but his body is rejecting a lot of it. He reminded us tonight that he had only taken three bites of food all of yesterday and only two today.

Bill Logue called from Waco today, and Jim Caldwell called from Memphis. Jim and Norma will be coming over to Little Rock tomorrow. Jim has a great deal of compassion.

Jean and Bobbie Lee came over last night, and Bobbie Lee went back today. Jean's husband, "Hoss," will come over tomorrow and take Jean back if Tommy is still okay.

October 14, 1972

GOING HOME

Our Tommy went home today. He was tired and needed to go home. I think he really knew that he was getting near because the last two nights he had wanted us both to sleep in the room with him. Last night he would not take his pain medicine or his sleeping medicine, and so he talked a lot during the night. My only regret is that one time I said during the night, "Tommy, if you don't take your medicine you are not going to sleep much." I must have said it in such a way that it stung him a little.

I guess it was after that he asked if I thought he should stay in the position he was in. I asked him if he was comfortable and he said he was. I do not think he was really comfortable, because in a minute I heard him whispering to Ethel to move him. He did not want to bother me anymore. In fact, he insisted that I go on back to our bedroom and get some sleep. Later, Ethel awakened me and told me to lie in the room with him while she fixed breakfast. We had a beautiful conversation, and I apologized for being short with him. There is something beautiful that I lost in our conversation. I have tried really hard to recall it, but I can't.

This morning, he told me he was hurting so that he wished he could die. It was after breakfast that his wish was answered. He took a few bites of banana while I held him with my head up against his. I could hear him chew the banana, and he really seemed to enjoy it. He took several swallows of milk and then asked to urinate. It was while I was helping him urinate that he passed away. Ethel asked me to run call the doctor and I did. I really do not know how many minutes elapsed before I started mouth-to-mouth resuscitation, but I do not think it was any more than the three minutes which they say should not pass. And so, with no experience whatsoever, I started mouth-to-mouth resuscitation, really not wanting the Lord to bring him back to a life of pain. He had this thing about men showing affection to other men, and very seldom did I ever kiss him on his lips. I do not guess I have in years and years and years. But perhaps for a hundred times, I got to kiss his sweet lips.

Yesterday, Sunday, he let me rub his legs a lot. Three different times, I think, he said to me, "Hi, Dad." Each time I replied by saying, "Tommy, that is worth ten thousand dollars to me." One time, in the afternoon, he said, "Daddy, I love you." Then I said, "Tommy, that is worth ten billion dollars to me!"

It is almost midnight now and it has been a rough, tough day. The hardest people to greet were Tommy's friends. They have been so loyal to him. It was especially hard when Jon Poteet came, the young man who would take him from class to class at Parkview, and David Bauman, who had done it at Parkview also before he was transferred to Central. Also, Mike Teal came by. Mike has some physical difficulty himself, and he said, "I come by to give you my heart."

Reza Mobarak, from Iran, stayed with us last night, and I think the Lord planned that also. He has had the hardest time emotionally accepting Tommy's death. He was eating breakfast at the table when I ran in to tell him, "We've lost our boy." Reza, from across the world, has been part of our family. It was he who gave Tommy his only job. How proud Tommy was to make money, the only money that he really earned himself.

"Lord, You know I want to talk to Tommy more tonight than to You. And you know, Tommy, how much we miss you. A big part of my reason for living has gone. So I need your help, and the Lord's help. Momma and I both have missed you so badly, but we wouldn't call you back for anything. I am fixin' to turn in. I won't be hearing you call me tonight to turn you, and I'll miss that. It's not that I wasn't tired lots of times. You know that everything I could do for you brought me joy. Good night, Tommy. Good night, Lord."

October 16, 1972

FRIENDS TO THE END

The funeral service was beautiful, I thought. It was a real worship experience, with the singing of two triumphant hymns and a good, good sermon. James Street, a former pastor, helped Jerry Wilcox with the service.

Tommy's close friends were his pallbearers:

> Jonathan ("Bucky") Poteet
> Ritter Arnold
> Mike Teal
> Bryan McKinney
> David Bauman
> Randy Miller
> Delta Anderson
> Bill Farmer

Marilyn, one of the Pharis twins, friends in the neighborhood, at school, and at church, read the scripture.

The love and warmth of friends at the cemetery was a foretaste of what reunion must be in the next life.

October 17, 1972

BEING

People have been so good to come by and to "be."
Somehow, the fewer words said the better. Theological
discourses are so out of place. Telling someone that a young
man's death is God's will is not helpful. I have wanted to tell
those few who have suggested this that they need to read Leslie
Weatherhead's Will of God and meditate on Jesus' statement in the
model prayer: "Thy Kingdom come, Thy will be done on earth as
it is in heaven." This verse says to me that God's will is not
always done on earth.

And telling someone that God "needs" a person in heaven
more than we need that person on earth reflects a poor concept of
God. But people mean well; they are trying to be helpful. Our
loss has taught me that churches do need to teach people how to
visit those in bereavement. At least I know better now what not
to say.

John Russ and William Echols, former students at Henderson
State, came by the house. Dick Bumpass came all the way from
Annapolis, Maryland, Ed Drake came from Dallas, the Roselles
from Nashville, and all our kin from Texas and from West
Memphis. Many people like these said almost nothing, but their
presence and their touch said everything.

Don Hammonds, from Atlanta, purposefully delayed coming
several days. He and I have had good walks and talks in the
woods.

How can people make it without friends?

October 23, 1972

IN THE SPRING

Jerry Wilcox, our pastor, has been such a special friend to Tommy. They played so much chess together, and Jerry did a beautiful job with the funeral, telling stories about Tommy that made all of us laugh.

After Tommy's death, he told us about the last time they played chess together. Tommy, Jerry said, always won and had him beat in that final game, but missed an obvious play that allowed Jerry to win instead.

When Jerry left the house, Tommy gave him, Jerry thinks, his final good-bye when he said, "I'll see you in the spring."

November, 1972

PARKVIEW HIGH SCHOOL

Yesterday, I received an invitation from Parkview High School to preach the Baccalaureate service for Tommy's graduating class. I'm highly honored, more than anything I have ever been asked to do in my life.

Ethel doesn't think I can do it. She thinks it would be too hard on me emotionally, but recently I have been able to mention Tommy in sermons.

The main reason I want to is because I think Tommy would want me to. I must make my decision today.

March 18, 1973

BACCALAUREATE

It's actually one hour and 37 minutes past midnight and really May 28, but I wanted to date this the day of Tommy's baccalaureate.

I have driven to Fayetteville with Don Norrington and Jack Kimbrell for a meeting tomorrow.

The service was in the gym and went okay. I had to fight back the tears during the music. I used as much humor as possible in the talk. When I could underscore a point with humor, I did so in order to keep control of my emotions.

Don and Jack are upstairs at the BSU Center, and I'm downstairs by myself. I see Tommy in that gym for the service, over and over again.

I mentioned Watergate. I think Tommy would have had me talk about it. I stated my feeling that some people's reaction in Little Rock was as regrettable as some people's actions in Washington.

"Tommy, you couldn't have gotten down all those gym steps to the floor today. Someone would have had to take you in another way.

"The Carmelite nuns were praying for us, Tommy, Sister Marie Joseph tells me.

"By the way, Ethel told me that a big rat ran across the top of the gym and that's the laughter I couldn't understand once or twice. I dropped by the convent afterwards. When I told Sister Marie Joseph about the rat, she told me that you had arranged the distraction to keep my emotions in control.

"Ethel came back from Memphis, where she'd been with Louise after the removal of two wisdom teeth Saturday by our good friend, Joe Hall Morris. She's tough, isn't she, Tommy? I don't think she cried any today. I guess you noticed my voice didn't crack until the last when I called your name and that of Charles Williams, the black boy in your graduating class who drowned.

"Oh! son, how I miss you, my namesake, my joy, my comforter. How often you affirmed me and loved me. I miss being kissed and kissing you, touching you, loving you. Good night, son."

May 27, 1973

GRADUATION

It is now 15 minutes past midnight. This was the night of Tommy's graduation. Ethel and I debated about going, but we both realized that we wanted to go, though painful we knew it would be. The marches the band played were the same as those played at the baccalaureate last Sunday. The same march for coming in and the same march for going out were used again tonight. Ethel and I both saw in our mind's eye Tommy being rolled in and his being rolled out. I was very conscious, however, of his name not being called between the names of Donnie William Logan and Alfred Lowe.

The service tonight was pretty hard emotionally on both Ethel and me, especially when some of Tommy's favorite friends were given their diplomas, and when the Tommy Logue Memorial Award was announced as going to Jonathan Poteet, the young man who was Tommy's best friend, the one who pushed his wheelchair from class to class. It was also very difficult to bump into Chuck Bishop as we left the coliseum. He also had helped Tommy get around at school. Dexter Reed, the basketball star, called me by name and shook my hand. Chrissy Hightower had given us a hug as we walked in. She was the editor of the school paper and had written a beautiful editorial about Tommy. Then afterwards, we saw Mike Teal and Bryan McKinney and Lewis Pearson, the boy who wrote the beautiful article on Tommy in the school paper. Mike will be going to Hendrix, Bryan to the Naval Academy in Annapolis, and Lewis will be going to Vanderbilt on a writing scholarship.

No one came to be with us after the service. People flooded our house when Tommy died, and yet tonight I needed someone more than almost any time. We invited Rezy to go with us, but he had some appointments. But we did have a good conversation on the phone after it was all over.

Tim and John didn't go with us, just as they didn't go to baccalaureate. I really wished for them. I also wished for Louise. I wanted to call her tonight in Memphis and chat with her and tell her how we felt, but Ethel thought it would make us both cry.

"Tommy, I don't know what it would have been like if you had been here tonight. I know you would have wanted to go to the parties, and we'd made sure you got there. But we wonder if you would not have been depressed -- depressed that all the joys and thrills of high school were gone. Lewis Pearson is right. You savored every drop.

"I'm very tired, Tommy, and so I want to hit the bed. Again, I want to tell you how much I wish you would call us during the night to ask us to turn you over. But I know that that is gone forever. Good night, Tommy."

June 1, 1973

SHENANDOAH

It is about midnight. Tim leaves tomorrow for college. He has been playing on his guitar a tune he often plays, but which I do not know. Also, he has been playing "Shenandoah" on his french harp. It is a sad tune to me because of my association with the show by the same name. The three boys and I saw "Shenandoah" together.

I know that Tim will be only 150 miles away, but it is probably the ending of a daily relationship. He has been so much fun to live with. He has been out of his cast two days and has a bad limp. It is supposed to be gone in three weeks.

I guess this is another event that would be hard on Tommy -- tough to see his brother leave and tough to realize that he could never do the same himself.

The only good part in Tim's departure is the fact that John will be receiving more attention than at any time in his life.

"God bless you, Tim. Keep your smile, your sense of humor, your warmth, and your concern for the poor and hungry people of the world. I love you, son."

September 8, 1975

AND THIS IS LOVE

Tonight, at the Installation Banquet at our Leadership Training Conference, Arkansas Tech was in charge. In a beautifully executed service, all campus directors were placed behind their seated presidents, and I was placed behind the new state president, Paul Faulks of Arkansas State University. In the litany that everyone shared, we were instructed to wash the students' feet as Ken Medema sang "And This Is Love." Southern Baptists did not practice foot washing, but it was a moving experience for me as I removed Paul's shoes and socks and washed his feet, dried them, and then began the difficult task of getting his socks back on.

Then it hit me. I had not tried to put anyone's socks on since the last time I dressed Tommy. Instant flashbacks brought pain, tears, and a tenderness that I had long forgotten. I looked at Paul through my tears, conscious that he had no idea what was going through my mind.

May 19, 1977

A MAXWELL HOUSE COFFEE CAN

I'm leading a January Bible study at Southside Baptist Church in Fort Smith where my good friend, Steve Hyde, pastors. Steve let me change the format and speak on subjects I chose. One night, I spoke on silence and meditation. Another night, I talked about world hunger. Tonight's topic was grief.

I was telling the people about Tommy and saying that one of the best things we had done was to argue with school officials in order to keep Tommy in his regular classes. I explained that the way we solved the bathroom problem was to keep a Maxwell House coffee can in the boys' restroom. Tommy's best friend, Jon Poteet, gave Tommy the coffee can and emptied it after Tommy urinated each time.

Immediately, there was a voice from the audience. "I went to Parkview in Little Rock and I always wondered what that Maxwell House coffee can was doing in the boys' bathroom."

The congregation laughed, and I was thrilled to meet someone who had that connection with Tommy.

The incident has made me wonder where that old coffee can is now. Decaying in the Little Rock landfill?

The can would be a sacred thing to me now, and I wish I had preserved it as a trophy for Ethel and me, parents who fought to keep Tommy in regular school, living as full and as normal a life as possible. Even more, it would be a chalice, made sacred by a strong and loving friend who became arms and legs for one struggling to stay alive.

Undated

RETURN TO MOUNTAIN HARBOR

I'm back at Mountain Harbor, the place where Tommy asked me 20 years ago how long he had to live. Paul and Barbara Harvel have made their condominium available for me, and I am trying to put the finishing touches to the book.

The nights are cool, and the place is quiet and restful. As I sat on the deck tonight and looked at the stars in a totally clear sky, I asked myself again the meaning of Tommy's life and the meaning of grief. I still have few answers, but I do know that somehow in the crises of life, God builds in extra resources. Those things which we say we can not go through -- somehow we can and do.

I have dreaded this moment, the closing of the writing of the book. Finishing it, I now realize, was yet another death for me, and so I continued to put if off as if the book were the final, final good-bye.

But the time is right, and for the first time, I have read it through without a tear. Always before, I have wanted someone near, someone I could reach out and touch when I read through the tough pages. This time, I wanted to be alone.

"So tonight, Tommy, it's different. I've finished your story. What a beautiful example you gave your dad about the handling of life!

"So tonight, Tommy, it's a soon hello again. I will see you in the spring!"

Undated

Some of
Tommy's Poetry

THE LIGHT OF LIFE

The first warm flames descend and then ignite a slight
    fresh fire that burns a frigid face

deprived of sun which now returns to chase
The frozen frost away that stole the light
While wind, once piercing life with cold's
    dark blight,
Now dies away as summer's sparks erase
    the glacial fields and icy streams in a race
to heat and feed the earth before the night.

So like the earth, man's mind lets go
    and he again is gay and warm, as chilling
    thoughts
and snowy sighs give way to flowing love
and peace just like the streams now running free.

The Light of life, the sun, has come and caught
Us in a race.

Tommy Logue

GLORIOUS WATERS

Falling, whirling jewels,
Raindrops brilliantly smashing
    against stones,
Leaving freshness and brightness
    and air
Cool.

Streams, moisture quickly flowing,
Twisting and bouncing between
    boulders,
Throwing sparkling stars into space.

Liquid rolling off a ridge charging
    toward earth,
A thundering waterfall, unruly
    and wild,
Slamming against frantic waters.

A soft pond, a smooth sea,
The sun down, the wind
    gentle tugging,
A calm body of blue,
Tranquility.

Tommy Logue
June, 1972

The Author

as seen by his son, Tim.

ABOUT THE AUTHOR

(Tim's remarks at his dad's Retirement Supper)

Several people have mentioned Dad's frugality tonight, but you should all know that there is a sour side to it as well. When we were very young, Dad resorted to all sorts of measures to teach us that we ought to brush our teeth after every meal and snack. One summer, while we were at Ridgecrest, he was particularly zealous, and would often return to our cabin from a morning session and proclaim, "I'll give a dollar to anyone who's brushed his teeth." Sometimes it was only 25 or 50 cents, but that was still a lot to us kids. For some reason, though, we could never remember to brush our teeth. But one morning Mother wised up, gathered us together, and told us Dad would probably come in any minute and offer another prize reward for brushing teeth, so we all piled into the bathroom, did our duty, and waited for his return. In he came and, no doubt counting on our having forgotten as usual, made an unprecedented offer, "I'll give _five_ dollars to anyone who's brushed his teeth." We were ecstatic, and all of us -- Louise, Tommy, John and I -- piped up, "I have, I have, I have, I have." Suddenly, Dad's expression changed. Then, his frugality asserted itself again, and summoning up all his powers of biblical exegesis, he reinterpreted his first offer to mean he would _split_ that five dollars among all the children who had brushed their teeth. So instead of five dollars each, we each got a measly dollar and a quarter. And after that incident, he _still_ wonders why we all keep having cavities.

Despite what that story suggests, Dad has always been a very generous father -- generous with his time, with his money (usually), with his advice (especially), and with Mother's cooking. Practically every Sunday when we were growing up, he would whisper to Mother right after the benediction, "Ethel, there's a nice couple visiting from Benton today. Could you put down just two more plates for dinner? Don't worry about there being enough. I can eat peanut butter." He didn't always ask first, either. Sometimes, after turning off the lights at the church, he'd rush home to find Mother pulling the roast out of the oven and tell her he knew she wouldn't mind, but Mrs. So-and-So's husband was out of town so he'd invited her to eat with us. About the only thing he wasn't generous with was dessert -- especially chocolate pie -- because Mother wouldn't let him. If company threatened to consume our portion of this specialty, she'd hide it in the cabinet until Dad's generosity had spent itself and the guests were gone.

This generosity extended to our neighbors as well. Dad is particularly fond of taking care of other people's yards. When we first moved to Talmage Court, our only neighbors were the Hudsons, who had built their house only shortly before we built ours and whose lawn had just a few more blades of grass than ours. That first summer, Mr. Hudson made plans to lay down some good grass and had hauled in a truck load of dirt which stood in a pile in the yard, where it stayed for several weeks. Mr. Hudson, I suspect, was waiting for the heat wave to pass before he began spreading this dirt, but Dad got it into his head that we -- meaning, John and I -- ought to go over and spread that dirt ourselves, quietly, without saying a word to him. So for several very hot July afternoons, John and I lifted shovel-load after shovel-load of dirt, carrying it to every corner of the Hudson's very large lawn. We were entering our teens, at an age when we began to expect some recompense for our labor. Well, I think Tommy, who had overseen our efforts, persuaded Dad to pay us something for this work. But a day or two later, Dad learned that the Hudson boys, Jay and John, who were roughly the same age as John and me, were upset that we had preempted them, for evidently they were expecting their father to pay them for doing the job themselves -- when they got around to it. So, ridden with guilt, Dad tried to make amends and paid those Hudson boys for missing the chance to spread the dirt that his own, more fortunate boys did. Tommy could never figure that one out.

Like every respectable man of the house, Dad has always drawn a firm line between his professional and his personal life. More than anyone I know, he knows better than to bring the office home with him. Oh, sure, <u>occasionally</u> he could be heard making calls to colleagues late at night or on a weekend afternoon. But Louise is exaggerating, I think, when she claims that Dad severely limited her adolescent love life by tying up the phone for hours so that no interested male could get hold of her. Usually, he confined himself to dictating letters into his tape recorder, locking himself into his room, from which a steady drone could be heard, "Dear Jamie, comma, about that retreat, comma . . ." But when he really wanted to get away from it all, take the family on a vacation and leave student work behind him, then he severed BSU ties altogether. I faintly remember our spending two solid days in Hot Springs when we heard nothing of the BSU, though I could tell Dad was extremely restless: picking up the phone when it wasn't ringing, calling Mother "Coretta" (the name of his secretary), and yearning to ask the motel receptionist about group rates for BSU retreats. Only when we got into the car to head back home would he forget his vow. Driving out of Hot Springs or passing through some rural town we'd never heard of, he'd suddenly slow down the car and say, "Gosh, Ethel, we're only half a mile from Mrs. So-and-So's house. She did so much for the BSU in the fifties," or, "You know, I think So-and-So still lives in Brinkley. I wonder what he's doing now. We'll stop just a minute, just a minute. I think I can find his house." And eventually he would.

Despite all these contacts with the BSU world, I don't think we ever felt our family privacy was being intruded upon. On the contrary, Dad's work provided us with a sort of extended family, a network of close friends who compensated for our distance from the Logue and Garrott clans, both hundreds of miles away. It was exciting growing up with so many different sorts of people in the house: international students from all sorts of countries, like Rezy Mobarak (who still has an accent) or the African students who, after dinner at our Fairmont house, turned their forks over on the TV trays and started up a fantastic drum beat; friends like Paul Meers, who introduced us kids to Arkansas politics; BSU alumni from all walks of life; missionaries, like John Wickman, with stories from exotic lands such as India; the MIL Singers, a real rock-and-roll band to our undiscriminating ears; and the BSU directors and their families -- the Jamie Joneses, Neil Jacksons, and James Smalleys -- with children we could identify with, who shared with us the same problem of explaining to other kids just exactly what it was our fathers did: "He's a BSU director. A BSU director. It's sort of like a preacher, but he hasn't got a church." This BSU world didn't make us miss our Logue and Garrott kinfolk any less, but it helped to fill a void.

But the characteristic I've come most to appreciate in Dad is his affection, his instinctive affection. Several times in conversations with friends, when anecdotes have passed about our childhood and parents, these friends have asked me if I realize how unusual it was to have a father who wasn't ashamed to touch and hug his children, to express his emotions openly before them, to become a child himself again while among them. He knew how to discipline us, of course, but it wasn't easy for him to punish any of us. (Louise disagrees, but she grew up before Dad began reading Dr. Spock.) When we really misbehaved, he would feel compelled to assert his authority by threatening to use his belt on us. His voice would grow arch, then he'd march us into the bathroom, shut the door, and begin to administer justice. If he actually whipped one of us -- and occasionally he did -- he'd usually come to find us in ten minutes, smother us with hugs and kisses, and say he was sorry. But it was very hard for him to actually pull off that belt. I see him now, in that bathroom, fumbling and fumbling at his belt buckle, stalling for time, hoping that words would serve his purpose better than whipping . . . fumbling and fumbling with his belt.